THE CANADIAN
ROCKIES

Irving Weisdorf & Co. Ltd.

CONTENTS

Text by
Kara Kuryllowicz

Photography

AAA IMAGE MAKERS

Bill Gibbons	10b
Bob Hahn	26b
Reimut Lieder	27b
Bernie Pawlik	46b
Neal Weisenberg	31b
Bob Young	56b

BIRDS EYE VIEW PHOTO

Ron Garnett	front cover, 9b, 28/29, 35, 39
	46d, 53b, 57

FIRST LIGHT

Chris Harris	61a
Alan Marsh	60b
Steve Short/Palmer ATLA Can	22b
John Sylvester	18
Ron Watts	23
Larry Fisher	1, 6, 7, 8, 9a, 10a, 11a, 11b,
	13b, 16/17, 20a, 21, 25a, 26a,
	27a, 34, 36a, 36b, 37b, 38b,
	41a, 42b, 43a, 44, 45, 46c,
	47b, 51b, 60a, back cover
Paul Heppner	37a

THE IMAGE BANK

Guiliano Colliva	42a

MASTER FILE

Daryl Benson	50a, 64
Hans Blohm	55
Bill Brooks	24
Gloria Chomica	15
Graham French	56a, 62/63
Sherman Hines	43b
J. A. Kraulis	14b, 22a
Alec Pytlowany	12
Terry Parker	31a, 32b
Timothy Reynolds	4, 14a, 19, 25b, 41b, 58/59
Robert Tompkins	33a

VIEWPOINTS WEST PHOTOFILE LTD.

Johann Adlercreutz	20b
Paul Morrison	50b, 61b
Murray O'Neill	30a, 33b
Terry Parker	32a, 33c, 40, 48b
Bayne Stanley	38a
Kaj Svensson	3, 46a, 49

IRVING WEISDORF & CO. LTD. 5, 13a, 30b, 47a, 48a, 51a, 52, 53a

(Also available in French, German, Chinese and Japanese)

History of the Rocky Mountains

Offering some of the world's most dramatic mountain scenery, the Rockies have been recognized worldwide for more than a century. In 1889, British travel writer Douglas Sladen relied on the brand new Canadian Pacific Railway to reach the "**New Switzerland**".

While the prairies have long been plowed and "cow towns" like Edmonton and Calgary are proud purveyors of tourist attractions such as the West Edmonton Mall and the Calgary Stampede, the Rockies remain wild, rugged and largely uninhabited by humans.

The Rockies run from the Yukon Territories all the way south to Mexico. But, Canada is home to the highest, most spectacular peaks.

The Indians called these "**Shining Mountains**" theirs for at least 100,000 years. Explorer, Leguardeur St. Pierre, dubbed them "Montagnes de Roches" or Mountains of Rock in 1752, which although equally appropriate, is not quite so poetic.

Fiercely and loyally protected in one of the world's largest national park groupings, the Canadian Rockies are a much needed haven for entire mountain ecosystems. Since 1984, the United Nations has considered the **Banff**, **Jasper**, **Yoho** and **Kootenay National Parks** a huge (20,160 sq. km./7,782 sq. mi.) World Heritage Site. In 1990, **Mt. Assiniboine**, **Mt. Robson** and **Hamber Provincial Parks** were included.

*Lake Louise, in **Banff National Park**, is one of the Rockies' most recognized vistas worldwide.*

The Rockies follow the great Continental Divide, along the Alberta/British Columbia border, framed to the east by never-ending prairie plains and to the west by the rich, deep valley of the Rocky Mountain Trench.

In 1887, Banff National Park became Canada's first national park, two years after the area around the Cave and Basin Hot Springs was marked for development as a park and European style spa. Three years later, Banff National Park was enlarged to its present size of 6,640 sq. km. (2,564 sq. mi.). Other national parks followed soon after, Yoho (1886), Glacier (1886), Waterton Lakes (1895), Jasper (1907), Mount Revelstoke (1914) and Kootenay (1920).

Only those who "need to reside" in the parks actually live there, for example, employees of the parks and vital services. As all parkland is Crown-owned, homeowners, businesscs and hotels lease their lands from the Canadian Parks Service and pay annual land taxes.

Beloved worldwide, Banff, Jasper and Waterton Lakes on the east slope of the Rockies in Alberta and Kootenay and Yoho on the western slopes in British Columbia are the true Rocky Mountain gems.

The National Parks Act of 1930 ushered in the beginnings of the belief that animals should be protected in their native environments rather than in cages. Today, fences along the Trans Canada Highway help prevent roadkill. These may be extended to other roads and railways, but it was the first park wardens who killed "unwanted" wildlife by exterminating over 80 cougars in Banff and Jasper parks between 1924 and 1941. Even today, cougars are rarely seen in those parks.

After manipulating Rocky wildlife for decades, park managers are finally leaving well enough alone, in an attempt to let natural balances and cycles re-establish themselves. Lessons have been learned the hard way.

*Mount Rundle is the highest mountain peak in **Banff National Park**.*

Banff National Park

Serene lakes, sparkling streams, tumbling water-falls, narrow gulleys, forested valleys, flowered meadows and above it all, the mountains in all their glory.

Nestled amidst an array of natural wonders that ring the town like precious jewels, Banff's opulence and luxury are just moments from great wilderness and the option of primitive camping in the rugged outdoors.

When hot springs were discovered near what is now the **Banff townsite**, everyone wanted the springs for their very own. Of course, visions of potential profits pitted man against man and it became apparent only government intervention would get people to share these natural wonders.

In 1855, a small 26 sq. km. Federal Reserve was created around the springs and by 1930, Banff National Park's size was fixed at 6,641 sq. km. (2,564 sq. mi.). Lord Strathcona, a director of the Canadian Pacific Railway (CPR), christened the area "Banff" after his Scottish birthplace. It's also said the town was named for "Banffshire" the birthplace of the CPR's president George Stephen.

The area opened up when the railway arrived in 1883 and built the Banff Springs Hotel in 1888, the very first tourist accommodation.

*The town of **Banff** is a busy resort area in all seasons.*

Bow Falls is not one of the largest or most rapid falls in the Rockies, but it is certainly one of the prettiest in the spring as the ice melts away.

The trail from Banff to Lake Louise and north to Jasper through Roger's Pass to British Columbia was a long and dusty one. By 1920 a proper road connected Banff to Lake Louise and finally in 1940, the road reached Jasper, but it was 1962 before the Trans Canada Highway reached through Roger's Pass to British Columbia.

By the turn of the century, Banff boasted eight luxury hotels and dozens of shops, but it was still known mainly as a summer resort.

Sunshine Village, a holiday resort and ski area hidden in a high mountain valley, is accessible to the public only by Canada's longest gondola ride at 25 minutes one-way. Sunshine Meadows, one of North America's largest alpine meadows, during the sweet summer months, offers a first-hand look at this fragile, but awesome alpine environment.

The **Bow Valley** draws the most visitors, because it's the most accessible. It's the only valley in the park with a road running through it, the Trans Canada Highway. It's home to the CP Rail lines as well as wildlife that seeks shelter from the harsh mountain winters here, with elk, mule and white tail deer, as well as big horn sheep attracting a variety of predators.

Follow the **Bow River**, a rolling, muddy torrent during the spring floods, but a gentle flow of placid, turquoise by late summer, across the graceful Bow River Bridge, through a rocky gorge until the river crashes more than 10 metres at **Bow Falls** to a frothing pool.

Conceived as a make-work project during the Great Depression, the Banff Administration Building went up in 1936. Respected architect Harold C. Beckett believed that buildings and their landscapes must complement one another and created the Cascades of Time, now known as the **Cascade Gardens**.

*Since 1888 when the **Banff Springs Hotel** was completed, it has offered thousands of visitors great service with a magnificent view of the Rockies.*

The gracious old dowager, the **Banff Springs Hotel**, highlights the natural wonders of the Rocky Mountains and the sound of Scottish bagpipes often echoes off the mountains' faces as dusk falls in a true Banff Springs tradition.

Banff Springs Golf Course, picturesque but terrifically challenging, is a magnificent alpine golf course that boasts 27 holes made up of three nines that play together, while maintaining the original appeal of the rolling tree-lined fairways and manicured greens.

*An aerial view of **Bow Valley** with Mt. Rundle on the left and the Banff Springs Hotel in the background.*

The **Town of Banff** sits in the shadow of **Cascade Mountain**.

Cascade Mountain was referred to by the Stoney Natives as their "Stoney Chief."

The **Upper Hot Springs** and the **Cave and Basin Springs** each have a unique character, with individual flow volumes, chemical composition and temperature. The Upper Hot Springs have a distinctive scent due to the water's high sulphur content. A "hot" property then and now, even the most jaded visitor lets the heat of the springs soothe aching bodies and tired minds.

These springs were a rare and special treat when the wild west was bereft of plumbing back in the late 1800s, but souvenir hunters who should have known better stole the stalactites.

The **Sulphur Mountain Gondola Lift** starts beside the Upper Hot Springs, which from the summit, offers a spectacular view of the Banff townsite and Bow River Valley. Ride to the top in a glass-enclosed, four-passenger gondola for a 360-degree view of Banff and the area.

Banff's mountains and lakes offer some of the most breathtaking spectacles in the world. **Cascade Mountain** dominates the Banff horizon, with its namesake ray of liquid silver always bursting from the rocks, high above the valley floor.

The **Vermilion Lakes**, are three shallow lakes, backlit by spectacular, almost surreal prairie sunsets, and are home to elk, mule deer, and coyote as well as muskrat and moose.

And **Mount Rundle**, a wave of solid limestone, soaring 1,500 metres high above the **Bow Valley**, stretching from the old mining town of Canmore to the very edge of the Banff townsite.

*Discovered by two CPR employees, William McCardell and Frank McCabe, the **Cave and Basin Hot Springs** almost became the downfall of this beautiful area until the government stopped its environmental and commercial abuse.*

◄ *Looking down into **Banff Valley** from **Mount Norquay***

*A view overlooking the **Bow River** to the south side of Banff.*

***Num-Ti-Jah Lodge** on Bow Lake.*

Vermilion Lakes is actually a collection of three small lakes.

Johnston Canyon, between Banff and Lake Louise, is an incredible example of centuries-old granite formations.

Other fascinating rock formations in the Rockies are the Hoodoos pillars.

➤

But besides the majestic vistas are the strange sights such as the intimidating, inhospitable, incredibly fascinating **Hoodoos**, strange earthen pillars that guard the south side of **Tunnel Mountain**. The Indians thought they were giants who slept by day and woke at night to stone unsuspecting travellers.

Lake Minnewanka or **Lake of the Water Spirit**, is lovely but lethal, with pristine blue waters that bring on hypothermia in mere minutes.

*A beautiful sunny, brisk day at **Peyto Lake**.*

Lake Louise Region

Lake **Louise** is set like a precious jewel in a valley ringed by **Mount Victoria**, **Fairview Mountain**, **Mount Lefroy**, **Mt. Whyte** and **Mount St. Piran**. The Stoney Indians believed thunder rose from the emerald depths of their "Lake of Little Fishes", but it's more likely the vast glaciers clinging to the mountains' steep slopes sent thunderous sounds reverberating through the valley as great chunks of ice crashed down.

In a shack bearing the misspelled sign "Sumit Hotel", A.P. Coleman spent a night at the end of the CPR track in May 1884. After paying for his bed in advance, he climbed into bunk No. 2, in the common guest chamber. A few hours later, another man, fresh from the pub, snuggled in beside him. Apparently, his half-dollar paid for only half a bed and a shared grey blanket. When he returned in 1907, he found a "comfortable hotel", the predecessor of today's lovely, elegant **Chateau Lake Louise**. Banff Springs was known for its grandeur and elegance, while CPR's revolving doors were the only effective means of keeping exuberant, freedom-loving guests on horseback out of the Chateau's lobby.

Gazing at **Mount Victoria** from a secluded spot highlighting the beauty of Lake Louise nestled at its foot, spot Victoria's **upper and lower glaciers**, once part of a massive glacier that filled the **Bow River Valley**. Today, meltwater from the glaciers fills the basin carved by the glacier to create the lovely Lake Louise.

***Lake Louise** changes colour with climate shifts - all part of the Rocky Mountain magic.*

*Seemingly perched on a hill-side, **Lake Agnes Teahouse** is a welcome resting point for weary visitors.*

A 3.5 km. trail climbs from the shores of Lake Louise past **Mirror Lake**, then **Bridal Veil Falls** to **Lake Agnes** named for the wife of Canada's first Prime Minister, Sir. John A. Macdonald, who visited the lake in 1886. From **Lake Agnes Teahouse**, the tantalizingly tempting aromas of homemade treats fresh out of the oven tempt hikers and horseback riders, luring them up the trail with visions of these delectable goodies. Sitting and contemplating the trails just travelled and the spectacular view from a comfortable spot - it's a simple, but special pleasure.

*It's not just plain sailing on **Lake Louise**! Lake Louise became very popular after two Olympic-class ski runs were built in the 1960s. But because of the area's beauty, visitors enjoy spending more leisurely time here just taking in the scenery.*

Peyto Lake takes its name from one of Banff National Park's first wardens, Bill Peyto.

Eccentric and legendary guide, Bill Peyto camped in splendid solitude on his namesake's quiet shores, but even then, almost a century ago, he dubbed it "too crowded", as **Peyto Lake** extended its reach into the **Mistaya Valley**. Shimmering blue green in the light, the lake's unique glimmering colour is the result of fine particles of rock flour suspended in the water, refracting the blue green light spectrum.

*Beautiful **alpine flowers** set against a magnificent mountain backdrop.*

*The picturesque **Post Hotel** in Lake Louise.*

The narrow valley gradually opens up to present a widening panorama of lofty peaks, with **Mount Murchison** forming the massive south portal of the **North Saskatchewan River Valley** above **Saskatchewan Crossing**. Here five rivers blend their waters to form the North Saskatchewan, with water spilling from an opening in the solid rock face of towering Mount Wilson.

__Lake Louise__ is named after Princess Louise Caroline Alberta, the daughter of Queen Victoria of England and Prince Albert.

Castle Mountain, *looking much like a European castle, was originally named Mount Eisenhower after the American president and general, Dwight D. Eisenhower.*

Moraine Lake *sits against the backdrop of Wenkchemna Peaks, Stoney Native for* Valley of The Ten Peaks.

Castle Mountain, a turreted and castellate-type mountain, is reminiscent of the majestically imposing medieval castles of old Europe and was aptly christened Castle Mountain by explorer Sir James Hector of the Palliser Expedition in 1858.

Moraine is a lake of many moods, with minor shifts in weather and light changing the colour of the lake and the atmosphere of the valley. A sharp contrast to the serenity of Lake Louise, the close proximity of the glowering mountain sentinels give this scene a fierce ruggedness.

The Great Divide runs across the tops of the rugged peaks known as Wenkchemna Peaks, or Valley of the Ten Peaks, that sit behind the lake.

Brave visitors to Lake Louise *take a Canada Day plunge in the icy waters. There's more to the Rockies than just fun in the sun!*

Bow River's western shoreline washes against the feet of Crowfoot Mountain.

Water rushes through the Mistaya Canyon and down the picturesque Mistaya Falls.

*Snowy peaks reflect in the waters of **Bow Lake**.*

*Guests of **Chateau Lake Louise** are rewarded with magnificent views of **Lake Louise** and **Mount Victoria**.*

*Don't try to befriend a **grizzly** or black bear in the parks. They prefer not to mix with the tourists.*

Rockies Wildlife

Black and **grizzly bear**, **elk**, **deer**, **moose**, **Rocky Mountain goats** and **bighorn sheep**, **cougars**, **bobcats**, **snowshoe hares**, **hoary marmots** and over 220 types of birds, from the tiny **mountain bluebird** to the imposing **golden eagle** share their mountain refuge with those who take advantage of these mountains, leaving the trappings of modern life behind in the car parks.

The National Parks Act of 1930 ushered in the beginnings of the belief that animals should be protected in their native environments rather than in cages.

*Horns rather than antlers are one of the distinguishing features of the **sheep** and **goat** family.*

*A nocturnal feline, the **cougar** or **mountain lion** is the largest of the North American cat family.*

*Incredibly agile, **mountain goats** prefer the rocky, rugged terrain as their habitat.*

*An amphibious rodent, the **beaver** builds dams in which it constructs its nest or lodge.*

*Though it looks large and cumbersome, the **North American bison** can still move fast enough to scare away curious onlookers.*

Often called the "whistler" because of its shrill call, the **hoary marmot** is indigenous to the alpine areas.

Probably the most recognizable of the Rockies' wildlife inhabitants is the **black bear**.

A mother **moose** and its calf make a refreshment stop.

*An aerial view of **Jasper Park Lodge** and golf course.*

Jasper National Park

In early summer the **Sunwapta Pass** meadows are tinted with the brilliant hues of wildly delicate mountain flowers and the air is sweet and clear, cooled by its voyage over the great icefields resting atop rugged mountain crests barely visible to the west.

After the heated, ferocious arguments surrounding the ownership of Banff's hot springs and remembering the damage done to forests, waterways and wildlife, the government proclaimed the **Jasper area** a national park in 1907, before the railway companies could despoil the wilderness.

The town of "Fitzhugh" in 1911, became Jasper two years later and, even today, many buildings are of wood and stone, harmonizing with the surrounding forests and mountains. Not that long ago, **Jasper townsite's** population was easily two-thirds people and one-third bears, with few confrontations thanks to a live-and-let-

live attitude on the part of both species.

It can be hard to tell the difference between a black bear and a grizzly, because the colour of both grizzlies and black bears runs the gamut of shades of light brown and tan to darker brown and black. As a result, colour is a less than reliable identifying characteristic. The grizzly's most recognizable feature is the prominent hump over the shoulders and a concave face from forehead to nose. Hopefully, you won't be close enough to note the grizzly's long curved claws.

Covering 1.75 acres or .75,000 sq. ft. with 58 cabins available to accommodate more than 800 visitors, **Jasper Park Lodge** is still known for its "wheeled" service, with bicycling wait staff carefully balancing fully loaded trays as they provide the ultimate in room service. It's tradition and a fine one at that!

*One of the lesser known, but no less impressive peaks in Jasper Park is **Mount Kerkelsin** with the **Athabasca Falls** in the foreground.*

*Thought by the Stoney Natives to be a home for wandering spirits, **Spirit Island** stands tall in **Maligne Lake**.*

Now an internationally recognized cycling route, with just two major passes to climb and take-your-breath-away scenery rising around every bend, the north-south **Icefields Parkway** is one of two major roads through the park.

The most extensive Rocky Mountain icefield, the monumental **Columbia Icefield** covers about 325 sq. km. (125 sq. mi.) and is up to 385 metres (1,260 ft.) deep in some spots. About 100 years ago, the **Athabasca Glacier** covered the area the road now owns, but in 1873, the sun won the yearly battle, driving the glacier's "toe" back nearly two kilometres.

There's no mistaking what Jasper National Park is renowned for! Because of the numerous sightings of bears in Jasper, it seemed only appropriate that this large creature be immortalized in a "welcome to the park" fixture.

The **Columbia Icefield** is a terrain of glacial ice that enveloped
the northern regions of North America about 10,000 years ago.

*Tangle Falls cascades through its mountainous route and is united with the **Sunwapta River** on its way north.*

The mighty **Athabasca River** winds its way through the valley, owing its distinctive pale green "milkiness" to the silt the streams pick up as they flow down from the glaciers.

Carved and etched into the rock by the Maligne River, the awesome **Maligne Canyon** is 55 metres (165 ft.) deep, with self-guiding trails and picturesque foot bridges providing access to special views. A longer walk down the canyon crosses six bridges leading to the canyon river.

The glacier lakes that gave birth to the **Sunwapta River** careen through the two canyons that form the **Sunwapta Falls**, where river mist rainbows often hover above the canyon rim.

*Water rushes through the limestone walls of the **Maligne Canyon** to meet the course of the river.*

*Standing guard at **Mount Robson Park**.*

Climb aboard the **Jasper Skytram** to reach the top of **Whistler Mountain** which presents a spectacular panorama that stretches from the town of Jasper to the distant **Mount Robson**, about 80 km. to the west.

The icy crown of forbidding **Mount Robson**, also the Mountain of the Spiral Road, is an unforgettable sight, at 3 954 m., the highest of Canadian Rockies.

Listen carefully at the water's edge and you may hear water swirling through distant subterranean tunnels, as **Medicine Lake's** waters rise and fall, creating an enchanting summer lake in the warmer months, but leaving little more than muddied clay flats as the leaves turn to gold and the snows blow in. It may look beautiful to the tourists but the Stoney Natives were afraid of this phenomenon and referred to the lake as bad medicine!

◄ *At 3 954 metres, **Mount Robson** is the highest peak in the Canadian Rockies.*

*What more appropriate name than **Medicine Lake** for this calm and reflective body of water.*

*A storm breaks over **Jasper National Park**.*

*A beautiful view of the Rockies from **Jasper Park Lodge**.*

*Named after World War I heroine, **Edith Cavell**, this mountain is best known for its mountaineering challenge.*

A fitting tribute to Edith Cavell, this singular peak shines brightly on sunny days, but **Mount Edith Cavell** has also had its sombre moments, often hiding behind clouds as it listens to the thunder of ice and rock falls. In October 1917, the enemy executed this British nurse for helping allied soldiers escape occupied Belgium during World War I.

A relaxing easy 8 km. (5 mi.) trip is a scenic three-hour walk in the **Valley of the Five Lakes**, on a trail looping around five small lakes nestled at the foot of the **Maligne Mountains**.

Maligne Lake, this picture-perfect body of water, earned its ominous name thanks to the treacherous currents that lurk near its junction with the **Athabasca River**. The lakes sparkling emerald, turquoise and amethyst hues are the result of light refracting off the rock-flour particles floating in them.

*The **Maligne Valley**, where gentle streams can quickly turn into raging, surging waterways.*

*So aptly named, **Emerald Lake's** remarkable colour is the result of suspended rock-flour particles.*

Yoho National Park

Yoho - the Cree use it when expressing wonder or astonishment in Cree and with its apt "rock-walls and waterfalls" motto, this British Columbia park is most deserving. With waterfalls, lakes and relatively speedy access to the upper subalpine and alpine ecoregions, hiking the Yoho Valley gives visitors a real taste of the Rockies' many facets and diverse ecosystems.

Native Cree for "It's wonderful!", spectacular **Takakkaw Falls**, one of Canada's highest waterfalls, is fed by the meltwaters of Daly Glacier. Four local climbers successfully scaled the frozen Takakkaw Falls, heralding the debut of waterfall ice climbing as a significant winter activity in the Rockies over two decades ago.

A Canadian Heritage River since 1989, **Kicking Horse River's** ever-charging braided stream is one of the world's biggest gravel producing rivers.

1882 was a monumentous year for Canadian Pacific Railway surveyor Tom Wilson. He discovered Lake Louise, then crossed Bow and Howse Passes, found ore on the slopes of **Mount Stephen** and topped it off with **Emerald Lake**. When his horses sought greener grasses, Wilson tracked them across **Natural Bridge** to this other gem of a lake, which became Emerald when Lake Louise, nee Emerald, was renamed in 1884.

Takakkaw Falls are North America's highest falls.

44

*Like an alien spacecraft's landing site, these **Paint Pots** are a natural phenomenon of richly tinted soils.*

*Fossils were discovered in 1877 and the **Mt. Stephen Fossil Bed** and its trilobites have become world famous.*

Natural Bridge, *another wonder from Mother Nature's Rockies Collection.*

*The **vegetation** and **flora** in the Rockies changes with altitude and elevation.*

*Autumn comes to the **Lake O'Hara** area of **Yoho National Park**.*

*A Canadian Pacific train enters the **Spiral Tunnel** pass.*

Fragile, delicate and extremely vulnerable to human-kind, the number of visitors to the **Lake O'Hara** area is controlled in an attempt to protect the precious subalpine vegetation.

At one time, the **Kicking Horse River** would have created a charming waterfall as it hit the rocks, but over the years the powerful waters have worn a narrow channel creating their own passage, the **Natural Bridge**, which is completely covered at high water.

*The grandness of the park's mountainous scenes are softened by the brilliant colours of the Rockies **flora** and the elegance of its **wildlife** inhabitants.*

Kootenay National Park

Although its natural wonders possess their own unique charm, they're often overlooked by those seeking the more spectacular, less subtle wonders of the better known parks like Banff and Jasper.

Established in 1920, Kootenay National Park owes its existence to the burbling **Radium Hot Springs** that coat the walls of **Sinclair Canyon** in the Columbia River Valley with steam from its 38°C (68°F) waters.

The Sinclair Canyon looms above the welcoming deep heat of the Radium Hot Springs, with examples of rock art left by natives who also used the springs almost a century ago.

In July 1968, much of the forest in **Vermilion Pass** was consumed by fire when a bolt of lightening set the forest alight, consuming over 2,400 hectares in just four days. While the landscape appears devastated, fire is an essential process which regenerates the land and inspires new growth.

Once past their prime, forests are supposed to burn. In the montane ecoregion, natural fire return cycles are in the order of 42 to 56 years, in the lower subalpine 77 to 130 years and in the upper subalpine 180 years. Forests that are much older are in decline, providing a good habitat for relatively few species. The absence of major forest fires is marked in the national parks during the past 50 years, and much of the vegetation is now over-mature. It reduces wildlife range, while creating huge dry areas that are essentially giant tinderboxes.

Like forest fires, the avalanches that roar unchecked down mountain slopes destroy all life, but they create ecological diversity, with meadow shrublands and edges that become home to other species who can forage there year round.

The Mitchell Range forms the eastern border of the south half of British Columbia's Kootenay National Park. These ranges are characterized by "...torturously folded and intricately faulted shale..."

Two of the highest peaks in the Mitchells are Mt. Harkin at 2 982 metres, and Mt. Daer at 2 941 metres. Both are visible from highway #93 which traverses the park. They form a magnificent backdrop to the turquoise-coloured **Kootenay River**.

*The **Tokumm Creek** created **Marble Canyon** in 8,000 years, carving a chasm 600 m. long and 36 m. deep.*

Sunrise illuminates the mountain peaks.

*Though delicate looking, the **Indian Paintbrush** is a hardy alpine flower.*

Mt. Lorette with the **Kananaskis River** in the foreground.

Kananaskis Country

A multi-use area, incorporating three provincial parks, **Peter Lougheed**, **Bow Valley** and **Bragg Creek**, there are over 3,000 auto-accessible camp-sites in some 20 campgrounds. Kananaskis was a native commemorated in local legend and the word has two meanings, "man with tomahawk in head" and "meeting of the waters". The **Kananaskis River** and **Bow Rivers** merge near **Bow Valley Provincial Park**.

*Nakiska was developed at **Mt. Allan** in Kananaskis Park for the downhill events at the 1988 Winter Olympics.*

Mt. Kidd *was named after a local storekeeper, Alfred Kidd.*

Kananaskis Village, is a world-class destination resort with three fully-appointed resort hotels as well as complete indoor and outdoor recreation facilities.

Adjacent to Kananaskis Village, the **Kananaskis Golf Course** was designed by the world recognized Robert Trent Jones, who called it the "finest location I have ever seen for a golf course".

The alpine or downhill skiing events are always a real highlight at Olympic Winter Games and back in 1988, the world focused on **Nakiska** at **Mount Allan**, the site of all alpine events. The entire Nakiska facility was built specifically for the Olympics and because the Chinook winds common to this area can cause air temperatures to rise by more than 20° C, Nakiska has extensive snow-making capabilities. Chinook is an Indian word that means "snow-eater". The 1988 Winter Olympics are also fondly remembered for the appearance of the Jamaican Bobsled team, who inspired the Disney movie Cool Running starring Canada's own, the late great John Candy.

Mount Kidd was named for John Alfred Kidd, a store manager, who lived nearby in the tiny town of Morley.

Mount Lorette was named after a mountain range in France.

In 1988, Calgary hosted the Olympic Games and **Canmore Nordic Centre** hosted the nordic ski events and features 56 km. of cross-country ski trails that are used for hiking, mountain biking and interpretive walks in the summer.

*As the moon crests over **Mt. Elpoca** the peaks resemble a lunar skyline.*

*The **Kananaskis Country Golf Course** also offers skiing facilities in the winter months.*

Waterton Lakes National Park

The scenery demands a certain respect, commands a definite reverence as the sweeping prairies roll golden against the rugged, reaching mountains. Dramatic transitions and a bold study in nature's own contrasts... **Waterton Lakes**, where balsamroot and prairie crocus bloom and kestrels soar, while bear grass and mountain herbs cover alpine meadows and eagles ride the summer thermals, hovering for endless airborne moments

Of confirmed eccentric, explorer and naturalist Charles Waterton, Theodore Roosevelt once said he was the first field naturalist to ever write of "the magic and interest, the terror and beauty of the far-off wilds".

The MV International, a 22 m. long (72 foot long) passenger boat which cruises Upper Waterton Lake, is a beloved summer institution.

Well into summer, snow lingers on **Mount Custer** just inside the state of Montana, helping to feed **Cameron Lake** and keep it icy cold. Mount Custer's lush avalanche slopes are prime grizzly bear habitat, but the lake lies in a magnificent, bowl-shaped cirque, carved from the mountainside by a mighty glacier.

Waterton's peaks are multi-coloured, tinted in delicately-hued red, green, brown, violet and tan shades, unlike the greys that dominate the mountain slopes that lie to the north. A striking rainbow of colour is etched into the bedrock of **Vimy Peak**.

Upper Waterton Lake, the Rockies' deepest lake at 135 m(443 ft.), has its southern tip in Montana's Glacier National Park.

Red Rock Canyon *This canyon, in the upper* **Blakiston Valley***, cuts through a colourful floor of oxidized argillite, an ancient metamorphosed shale, to create this spectacular vision.*

*Like a mystical mansion, the **Prince of Wales Hotel** overlooks Upper Waterton Lake.*

After three years of drought, farmers were suffering and there was soon talk of putting a dam on the international waters between **Upper and Middle Waterton Lakes**. Back in 1919, that would have produced enough water to irrigate 75,000 acres of parched farmland. But American authorities wouldn't give their permission and worried park residents breathed a sign of relief. A dam was later build east of the park on the Waterton River.

Construction began on the **Prince of Wales Hotel** in the winter of 1926, but almost immediately, there were setbacks. Gusting Chinook winds blew the framework off-centre and the design was changed. Overlooking **Upper Waterton Lake**, the **Bosporus** and **Middle Waterton Lake**, the seven-storey Prince of Wales made its debut in 1927, a postcard-perfect landmark.

The Rockies...a place for all seasons

People live, work and come to play here in the Rockies because they can't imagine a view without mountains. Where else can you experience the magnificence of mountainous peaks, deep blue-green lakes and brilliantly coloured wild flowers? Where else in the world are there such fascinating natural formations or glacial plateaus? Where else can you ski, fish, hike, go mountain climbing in some of the most magnificent country in the world?

The Canadian Rockies, nature's winter and summer wonderland.

*A field of **wild flowers**...nature's own paintbrush.*

*The **wild rose**, Alberta's provincial flower.*

Flowers and Birds of the Rockies

Adding beautiful colour contrast against the silver-grey peaks and emerald-blue lakes the flora of the Canadian Rockies is elegant and delicate looking, yet extremely hardy and weather "resistant".

After manipulating Rockies' wildlife for decades, park managers are finally leaving well enough alone, in an attempt to let natural balances and cycles reestablish themselves.

*Rarely seen, but often heard, the **horned owl** shyly hides away from visitors who venture too close to his home.*

*So appropriately named, the **Indian Paintbrush** is indigenous to the alpine areas of the Canadian Rockies.*